Rue, Euro and the New Baby

By Clem King

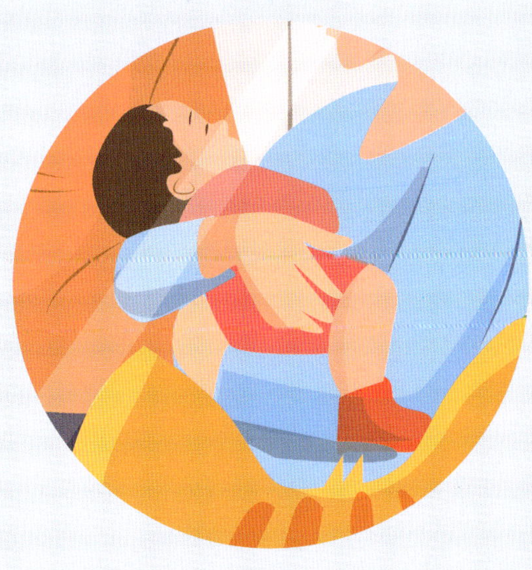

Rue and Euro had a nap
in the sun.

Euro stuck to Rue like glue,
all the time.

“Too close!” yelled Rue.

Euro shifted away,
feeling blue.

It was time for tea.

Euro could not wait
to chew up his stew.

A drip fell from his lips.

“Ew! Do not get that on me!” said Rue.

Euro threw his hand up to his lips.

One day, Mum and Dad came home with a new baby!

"This is **bad** news!"
yelled Rue.

"Why?" said Euro.
"It's just a baby."

"You do not have
a clue!" said Rue.
"That baby will scream
all the time!"

"No!" said Euro.

It was true.
The new baby **did** scream!

Mum and Dad played music
and walked with the baby.
But still the baby screamed.

“Someone please rescue me!” said Rue.

“I’m going to the next room,” said Euro.

Euro sat.

Rue came, too!

Rue licked Euro
a few times!

Euro sat very still
so Rue would not stop.

There were no more cat and dog feuds!

CHECKING FOR MEANING

1. What did Mum and Dad bring home? *(Literal)*
2. Why did Rue say the new baby was bad news? *(Literal)*
3. How does Euro feel about Rue? How do you know? *(Inferential)*

EXTENDING VOCABULARY

ew	What does the word *ew* mean in the story? What word could the author have used instead of *ew*?
true	Which letters in the word *true* make the /ū/ sound? What is the opposite of *true*?
feuds	What does the word *feud* mean? What is another word for *feud*?

MOVING BEYOND THE TEXT

1. Do cats and dogs usually get along with each other? Do you think Rue and Euro will stay friends? Why?
2. Have you ever spent time around a baby? What are they like?
3. Have you ever had to get used to having a new sibling? What changed at home?
4. When Rue licked Euro, it was a sign of affection. How can you show affection to a pet? (Don't lick them!)

TIME TO WRITE

Imagine you are Euro in the story. Write about how you feel now that Rue likes you. What else might you and Rue do together now that you're friends?

PRACTICE WORDS